The Spiritual Whistleblower's

Break Up Manual: Volume 1

How to Defeat a Narcissist

Chanel Jasmin Clark

Kill Jezebel Media, LLC
c/o C. Clark
PO Box 645
New York, NY 10272

ISBN-13: 9781983031489

Printed in the United States of America

Connect with the SWB

SpiritualWhistleblower.com
Facebook.com/SpiritualWhistleblower
Youtube.com/SpiritualWhistleblower
Instagram.com/SpiritualWhistleblower

This book is dedicated to my daughter Caress:

Mommy has taught you well. Learn from my mistakes, remember the life lessons from your past and take charge of your future! Remember to never live in dysfunction and to always safeguard yourself against toxic people. I've taught you how to use your gift of discernment. You were Heaven-sent to me from God because He wanted me to experience the real value of family and maternal love. We are spiritually connected and our bond is unbreakable. Thank you for protecting Mommy and always having my back. I promise to always do the same for you. #LoyaltyIsRoyalty

I love you Boomie! ♥

To Aunt Tamara:

I remember the day that you prayed over me and my daughter when she was only a few days old. That was 18 years ago. I want you to know that your prayer sustained me and Caress all of these years. Aunt Tamara I want to thank you so much. You are a prayer warrior and guardian angel. I love you.

"For we wrestle not against flesh and blood, but against principalities, against powers, against the rulers of the darkness of this world, against spiritual wickedness in high places."

— **Ephesians 6:12**

Table of Contents

Introduction

I cannot believe that I gathered up the strength to write this book. Honestly, I stopped trying to complete my goals for a while due to some unforeseen events that derailed my focus. I was too busy trying to help ungrateful people. While I was striving to be a great mother to a child with a mental disability, my enemies were plotting against me. I overlooked my own needs trying to support others who could care less about mine. The moment I became more selfish and enforced my boundaries, I was labeled the bad guy.

God has a funny way of directing us to our purpose, but we also have an obligation to meet Him there half way. All of my pain and life lessons have taught me what I've known in my heart all along: *that my power is in **"MY PURPOSE."***

That's right, my purpose. I am unique and very special. I am a child of God. I am kind, loving and compassionate. I have a heart of gold. As much as people have done me dirty, I cannot bring myself to treat people the same way. I only know how to stay true to who I am and keep it real. My character will not allow for me to do evil shit to others because I know that God is **ALWAYS** keeping tabs. I don't understand why Narcissistic people choose to live their lives hurting innocent victims, when they know that God is watching their every move. They may be able to hide their deceitful ways behind closed doors, but they can't hide it from God.

At this point in my life, I have decided to be of service to Jesus Christ by delivering His children out of peril. I want to spread His word to those who will listen. I want to defeat the evil all around the world. I want to spread love, light and peace. My vision will come into fruition as I help victims of Narcissistic abuse. This is my God-driven purpose.

Let me first start off by saying that I am not a licensed psychiatrist or therapist. I am a certified life coach currently pursuing a Doctorates in Addiction Psychology. I miraculously survived a very long string of abusive Narcissistic relationships. This is not only my niche, it's my life story.

My childhood was nothing to smile about. I was reared in a cesspool of domestic violence and instability. My parents, grandparents, siblings and random family members have a variable of "Cluster B" personality disorders which all have contributed to the family's dysfunction. The abuse I endured over the years was covert, insidious and malicious.

When I discovered what Narcissistic Personality Disorder was, I made it a top priority to start cutting ties with some of my immediate family members in order to save my sanity. No disrespect, but a lot of my family members are morally and spiritually bankrupt. The cycle of dysfunction within my family has been a never-ending hamster wheel of toxicity. I have been fighting to get off of this "hamster wheel" it seems, forever. I disconnected myself from my family indefinitely because I could not tolerate the dysfunction any longer.

It is from those past experiences that I have derived a passion for helping victims of Narcissistic abuse. Every Narcissist in my family nearly destroyed me. I was always the verbal whipping post and scapegoat child. Constantly being "fat-shamed" and degraded out of cruelty. The maltreatment I encountered was swept under the rug and hidden from the public eye.

Unfortunately, the on-going cycles of abuse I suffered, had transitioned over into my adulthood. I was not strong enough to detach myself from the trauma bond. I would continue to attract toxic men who reflected the same abusive characteristics as my Narcissistic parents. I had to cut that umbilical cord in order to facilitate my own growth. I had to figure out how to dismantle the embedded toxic programming within me that fueled my low self-esteem. I had to unlearn everything that my abusive parents taught me about romantic relationships. They were both too busy trying to destroy each other instead of displaying a positive example of unity, love and compassion in front of their children. My mother and father taught me that violence and abuse equates love through their fist fights and violent altercations. My parents would quarrel in public and wrestle in the streets no matter where we were. It was quite embarrassing and scary to witness this as a child. I remember my mother trying to run my father over with her car, with me and my siblings in the back seat (we were terrified). Here I am at 42 years old, still having nightmares about those awful memories that continue to haunt me every now and then. I suffered Post Traumatic Stress Disorder as a result of this lingering distress. The fact of the matter is, I was reliving "*their*" toxic marriage vicariously through my own toxic relationships. I hold myself 100% accountable for my decisions and I don't expect my parents to apologize for their lack of accountability for their poor choices. As much as their domestic violence messed up my outlook on relationships, I was still able to break the cycle of dysfunction in order to achieve inner peace for myself. I became a better parent than both of them combined. I was able to give my daughter the gift of emotional nurturing to restore the void that they left in me when I was a child. The pain and lessons were worth it. I have no reason to be mad at either one of them. I forgive them both. I am at peace knowing that I will never be able to have a relationship with my parents ever again due to their inability to accept responsibility for the pain and suffering that they have caused me. I cannot go back to that. I am in a healthy spiritual space and I don't intend on giving that up for no one. They are who they are and I am who I am. They will both have to face God one day and deal with the repercussions of their abusive behaviors that destroyed their family. I am free from it all. I am happy to announce that I am healed from my past. How do I know that I am healed? Well first off, I have forgiven all of my abusers. It took me a long time to learn how to forgive. It was very difficult. There was once a time when I was too bitter to forgive anyone. I cannot change my past, but I certainly can take control of my future. Now that I am aware of how Narcissism has plagued my family, I am strong enough to protect myself from their toxicity. I still love my family, but I can never return back to having any type of relationship with them. I have made peace with that and I wish them all of the best. I have forgiven myself. I can sit here comfortably without holding any grudges or resentment. I confronted those demons. I am not a victim anymore. I am a victor. My journey has taught me grace, resiliency and humility.

I will not forego my past experiences by ignoring the cries of victims of Narcissistic abuse who are in need of spiritual guidance. I will help free the teenage girl who is being sexually molested by her stepfather. I will work overtime to assist the battered woman who is trying to escape her violent, controlling husband. I will make it a priority to teach women around the world that they must practice self-care and self-respect before entering a relationship. I have a purpose to fulfill before I exit this earth. My job is to expose Narcissists and provide abuse victims with the necessary tools to heal properly. I am the Spiritual Whistleblower calling out corrupt people with toxic personalities and demonic energy. I will blow my whistle and blow your fucking spot up! Every Narcissist better run when they see me because I will waste no time exposing them to the world. Make no qualms about it, I will make **every** Narcissist feel my wrath!

After seeking my own therapy and binge-watching YouTube videos on Narcissistic Personality Disorder, I did a lot of research on people with Cluster B personalities and further expanded my knowledge of Narcissism.

I could never fully understand why certain members of my family, gossiped about me behind my back. I could never fully understand why my mother always made fat remarks about my body, making me feel ugly and insecure as a young woman. My mother never took the time out to teach me how to love myself. I had to learn on my own. She made it her business to remind me every day, that I will always be overweight. She constantly compared me to my younger sister. She continued to break down my self-esteem every chance she could get. I promised myself to be a much better mother than she was. There isn't a day that goes by that I don't tell my daughter how much I love her and how beautiful she is. I don't want my child to ever experience the pain I felt of knowing that I could never be pretty enough to make my mother stop criticizing me. She continued to break down my self-esteem behind closed doors.

I could never understand why I was sexually molested by my mother's second husband and she didn't do anything to protect me from him when I told her about the abuse. Matter of fact, she's still married to him even after she learned that he had fondled me repeatedly during the days she wasn't home. She was supposed to shield me from this predator, but she turned her back on me because she viewed me as her competition instead of her child. My mother failed me. She knows in her heart what type of man she married, but she chose him over me. He cheated on her with other women and she believed all of those stories (and wanted to fight the women he slept with), yet she completely blew me off when I told her he molested me. It took me a long time to forgive her for that. She will have to live with the fact that she chose a pedophile over her own child. May God have mercy on her soul.

I could never understand why my father would complain about the abuse he endured as a child at the hands of his own mother, but he would then turn around and "triangulate" me against my siblings. My father wasn't there for me when I needed him during my teenage years. I needed him more than anything, but he blamed my mother for pushing him away from me and my siblings. As a man, nobody should be able to come in between you and your children. Nobody. There is no excuse for skipping out on your children's lives. He didn't put in the effort when we needed him the most. Blaming my mother is the cowards' way out. At the end of the day, "child neglect" is a form of emotional abuse. My father didn't do his part to raise me. He is just as much to blame as my mother is.

My parents are both Narcissistic and/or Borderline Personality-disordered. They both play the same mind games of control and manipulation. They use their children as pawns to keep tabs on each other as if they're in some type of invisible competition. It's like watching them play a never-ending game of chess. They both relentlessly point fingers at each other for destroying our family instead of facing the mirror and pointing at themselves. I could never understand any of their toxic behavior up until now. I am a survivor of Narcissistic Abuse.

I have defeated countless demonic attacks over my life. I am still standing. Many people wouldn't have lasted a single day in my shoes. I am resilient. I came out of the fire unscathed. Don't fuck with me, because you will hurt yourself in the process. I am covered by the blood of Jesus Christ. You won't win this one, so don't even try it. I wasn't supposed to survive these attacks over my life, but I'm here to tell you that I did. I knew something was always "*off*" about my family, but I didn't know that there was a psychological term for it [**Narcissism**]. I can attest that I've been through a lot of battles in my lifetime, and I proudly wear all of my scars like a warrior. I could write a book about all of the physical and emotional abuse that I endured at the behest of my mother and father, but I rather invest my energy in being positive and helping innocent people escape abusive situations. I have an obligation to set a better example for my daughter. That time for me has come. The time is now.

I wish you all a lifetime of healing and peace. Whether you're currently in the midst of a nasty break up with a Narcissist or if you have ever tried to break free from a Narcissistic parent, you have my deepest sympathy. I'm here to tell you that it does get better. The healing is slow and arduous, but you will eventually learn how to maintain those boundaries in order to keep the antagonistic attacks at bay so that your healing can progress.

The Narcissist is one nasty, vile, uncouth, demonic piece of shit. An angelic saint to the public eye, but a toxic trouble-maker behind closed doors. They hide behind smoke screens in an attempt to control people's perceptions of them. They go to church and preach bible scriptures, but do their evil deeds when no one is looking.

I beg you to please guard your life and protect your spiritual space. Respect yourself enough to walk away from anyone who disrespects you and tries to destroy you the first time around. God bless you. I don't wish Narcissistic abuse on my worst enemy.

Go in peace.

~ CJC

What is a Narcissist?

A Narcissist is a toxic, impulsive, self-centered, shallow, non-empathetic unremorseful, deeply insecure, arrogant, dishonest, gossiping, two-faced, delusional, troublemaking, spiritually-tainted, envious, self-entitled egomaniac with extremely low self-esteem. You'll often find that Narcissists "subliminally" reside within the confinements of their own bubble world. It's all about THEM. It's never about YOU. But funny enough, they cannot survive without you! Their whole existence depends on the attention and tangible possessions you provide them. They present themselves to the outer world as morally good citizens, however, when they are behind closed doors, they are DEMONS. Low down, despicable, deceptive, soulless demons!

The constant mind games, backstabbing and hurtful shit that they do to innocent people are beyond sinister. No one deserves this type of treatment. It's inhumane and ungodly to destroy anyone emotionally. Victims are left struggling to break a toxic soul tie while dealing with an onslaught of health problems stemming from the Narcissistic abuse (i.e.: C-PTSD, stroke, high blood pressure, hair loss, lethargy and drug/alcohol addiction).

One can argue that this is a medical condition, however I have to somewhat disagree. When someone intentionally inflicts severe emotional pain on another person with no feeling of guilt or remorse, then it becomes an issue of sadism and spiritual assassination. The Narcissist is not operating from a place of love because he was denied emotional development and nurturing as a child. He cannot process emotions the same way that Empaths can. He continuously repeats the abuse he endured from his early childhood by abusing every woman he covets.

When describing the Narcissist, I deliberately left out the word "**emotional**" albeit, the Narcissist lacks empathy. But that doesn't quite mean that they aren't emotional beings. Their emotional compartment is hindered. I've seen Narcissists act out in full blown rage; some of them can become unhinged and throw temper tantrums when they do not get their way. So yes, they can be quite emotional but at the same time, they can also lack empathy while "appearing" to be emotional. They are able to mirror real feelings and real emotions of "real" empathetic people. They have the ability to cry real tears, but those tears aren't connected to anything spiritual or loving.

It's confusing isn't it? Like an oxymoron. Quite perplexing these empty creatures are. If you see a Narcissist cry, it's usually over something or someone that he has lost control over. They rarely cry over the loss of people unless those that are long gone have provided the Narcissist with a continuous source of income, sex or adulation/ attention. They are ALL liars, users, manipulators, serial cheaters, con artists and scammers. If you can't be used in some shape, form or fashion, then you are basically useless to the Narcissist.

Who can be considered a Narcissist? Well just about anyone can. Your mother, father, siblings, friends, pastor, coworker, supervisor. Anyone can be a Narcissist. These reptilians are everywhere and anywhere, right underneath your nose in close proximity. Beware and be careful. They move in calculated steps. Slithering snakes switching up their personalities like chameleons. The Narcissist's goal is to charm you and persuade you to get you to disengage your personal boundaries.

In the beginning when you first meet a Narcissist, he will pour on the delicious compliments and ass kissing as soon as you walk through the door. The Narcissist will treat you like a royal goddess and kneel before your feet. Once he reels you in for the kill, you're hooked. The Narcissist won't accept any type of rejection from you, however, he will have no problem rejecting you first. When he says yes, what he really means is "no" and when he says no, he will punish you if you demand any type of explanation from him. He must maintain the upper hand at all stages of your courtship. You will lose your sanity, your hair and your religion when you are done dealing with a Narcissist. He will constantly contradict himself and toy with your emotions all for the sake of garnering and securing your undivided attention (**Narcissistic supply**).

Narcissists are pathological liars. Habitual, repetitive, delusional liars. They talk in circles using "word salad" to keep you discombobulated and disheveled. Don't try to make sense of it because you can't. They lie for no reason. They lie because it feels good to them. They lie because they love the sound of their own voice. They lie because they enjoy the drama it brings once the lie has been exposed. They thrive off of deception. It's fuel. Your attention, admiration and adulation, provides them with **energy fuel**. The Narcissist's control over your emotions is like an orgasm to his ego. Pure venomous adrenaline!

Narcissists prey on innocent targets (people with kind and compassionate personalities). He views all empathetic women as weaklings and will treat each one like a cat cornering a mouse. Just like a cat, the Narcissist won't kill you right away. Instead, he will toy with you, slap you around and torture you before finishing you off. Narcissists are sadistic. They orchestrate your emotional pain and drink it like soda. They praise you on your way up, and laugh at you when you fall on your ass (*the Narcissist is usually the one that kicks the pedestal from under your feet*). Didn't I tell you that they were sadistic?

Most people will tell you to simply move on after a break up with a Narcissist, but it doesn't quite work like that. The Narcissist's "break up" consists of a nasty push/pull entanglement to prevent you from moving on. The Narcissist doesn't want you to break free from him emotionally. He thinks he is your puppet master and he's always going to set the stage to get an emotional reaction out of you (yes, even if he's in a new relationship with someone else). He will continue to stalk, spy and fuck up your life while he's chilling with the new woman he cheated on you with.

If you want go inside of the mind of a Narcissist, then keep reading. This shit gets real deep and if I can save your life and a few others, then I've done some justice in this world. Congratulations on seeking out the first steps to learning more about

Narcissism. You're reading this book because you're curious to learn more about Narcissism or you're either trying to make sense of your ex-boyfriend's insanity. If you're an Empath like me, then you're a good person and the Narcissist you once loved, came into your life like a tornado and tore shit up and walked away without a scar. They are masters at this shit. They have an incredibly long trail of human carnage and broken hearts behind them. They cannot stop the abuse nor do they want to. They thoroughly enjoy it.

If you are a toxic Narcissistic individual reading this book for the very first time, then I'm sure you will get offended or either laugh at the idea of you hurting others. It's not a laughing matter when you cause someone a great amount of emotional pain which can result in pushing your victim to have a

nervous breakdown or to either attempt suicide.
Dear toxic person, I don't hate you at all because
I'm smart enough to realize that the battle you're up
against is the battle within yourself. You're
fighting some serious demons. I'm sorry but you
are an emotionally-damaged toddler trapped inside
of an adult's body. You have no moral compass
because you refuse to see the error of your ways.
You love to hurt innocent people because somebody
you loved, abused you as a child. I want you to
keep reading this book because you may learn a
thing or two about your piss poor behavior and
insanity. I pity you.

Narcissistic Personality Disorder is listed in the
American Psychiatric Association's Diagnostic and
Statistical Manual of Mental Disorders, Fifth
Edition (DSM-5). There has been much

speculation as to whether or not Narcissistic Personality Disorder should be classified as a mental illness instead of a personality disorder because of the severity of the disease and its effects on victims. There is currently no cure for NPD other than death. Most, if not all Narcissists reject the idea of going to therapy for treatment due to their arrogant "above the law" attitude. Sadly, the Narcissist will die this way leaving behind many sabotaged friendships and relationships. By the time the Narcissist is old and gray, he will have destroyed all of his blessings because he cannot bring himself to break his own cycle of dysfunction. He stands in his own way and can't see himself out.

There are all types of Narcissists: Malignant, Covert, Overt, Cerebral, Somatic, Elite, Inverted, etc. This book will only discuss the surface of

Narcissistic abuse in romantic relationships. Most Narcissists are polyamorous and cannot be groomed or "loved" into having morals and integrity unless the situation benefits them to do so (*and that usually is short-lived*). The Narcissist is comfortable living in his dysfunction. He will spend his entire lifetime projecting fear and insecurities onto his idealized victims. By the time he's finished devouring you, the Narcissist will have successfully dismantled your self-esteem. His overall goal is to break your spirit in half and pull you down to his level. He will leave you numb until he circles back around and returns to abuse you some more.

There is even a biblical reference that ties the Narcissist to the Queen Jezebel, a woman who seduced and murdered many men. Just like the

Narcissist, Queen Jezebel was self-centered, haughty, heartless, egotistical, unremorseful, manipulative and deceptive. She didn't believe in Yahweh and wanted to destroy anyone who did. Narcissists deliberately harm spiritually-intuitive people, just as Jezebel did to God's prophets when she killed them off. Narcissists are fueled by the Jezebel spirit of manipulation, deception and sadism. They do not love anyone, not even themselves. They obsess over having power and control over their ex-lovers, which explains why they connect themselves to you spiritually through strongholds after the relationship has ended. If God is love, then anything that doesn't love God, cannot possibly love mankind. The Narcissist will hate you for worshipping God over him. He is demonic and he feels that he's greater than God.

To my precious Empaths, it's time to wake up. Become educated on Narcissism; learn the manipulation tactics and protect your spiritual energy. Self-care must become a priority or else you will succumb every time you attract a new Narcissist into your life. Stop allowing toxic men to overstep your personal boundaries! You will continue to repeat what you refuse to repair! Please remember to treat the Narcissist with compassion just as your Lord and Savior has handled you, but do this from a distance. Whether you're ready to forgive your ex-Narcissist or not, stay far away from him. He will continue to hurt you repeatedly if given the opportunity. He cannot be saved. You are his ex, not his personal savior.

Mommy Issues & Bisexuality

A Narcissist usually has a very sickening codependent relationship with his mother. Because she is a Narcissist herself, she coddles and cripples her son during his early childhood, using coercive abuse. She molds her son to tolerate her abuse at an early age by emotionally neglecting him, physically/sexually assaulting him and spoiling him (or a combination of all three). She rewards the abuse with attention and then takes it away from him again. By doing all of the above, she has taught her son that he can achieve anything in life by being a manipulative abuser when he becomes a man. She is a bully and a toxic enabler. She molds her baby boy into her perfect little "son-husband." She teaches him that abuse is really a form of dysfunctional love.

The Narcissist has a love/hate attitude towards his mother. On one hand, he hates her because she abused him as a little boy. He resents her for beating him and calling him a sissy whenever he cried. He hates the fact that she sleeps with multiple men (or cheats on the one that she already has). He sees with his own eyes, that his mother is a piece of fucking trash. On the other hand, he loves her because she gave birth to him. He feels obligated to show honor, respect and loyalty to her despite her manipulation tactics and abuse.

In her mind, she not only serves as his mother, but also as his surrogate wife, play sister and imaginary girlfriend all in one. This woman has literally fucked up her son's head. It is because of her Jezebel ways, that her son hates all women and secretly prefers men. If he hasn't tried to sleep with a man yet, he will be tempted to do so at some point in the near future when his curiosity gets the best of him. He views all women as abusive, lying whores and gold diggers, just like his mother. His Mommy-inflicted trauma runs really deep.

Whenever you see an older Narcissist in his 40s, 50s or 60s, continuously fuck up all of his past relationships, then nine times out of ten, it usually means that he doesn't like women. I mean seriously, what more could he ask for? Why hasn't he been able to secure a good wife and settle down? Why does he prefer hanging with his boys instead of his girlfriend? Why does he bash gays and bully women behind closed doors? Why does he hop from one bed to the next complaining that ALL women are the same? Why hasn't he checked his mother and told her to mind her fucking business?

Why won't he establish boundaries and make his mother respect you and your relationship? Why does his Mommy keep tabs on her son-husband as if he's a three year old little boy? Why hasn't she taught her son to be faithful to one woman and to settle down with one? Why won't the Narcissist cut that umbilical cord and move on from his Mommy?

It's because he's a closeted bisexual man and he is afraid to come out due to the backlash that he will receive for sleeping with men on the down low. That's why he has a reputation for being a whore around his boys, because he wants everyone to think he runs through women. He fools people into thinking that he craves pussy 24/7 but that's all a lie. No one would ever suspect him of wanting to get his dick sucked by another man or take one up his ass. He has to create a smoke screen to throw people's perception of him off. Any man that has a very long string of sabotaged relationships with good, wholesome women and can never settle down with just one woman, CLEARLY doesn't like women at all. The red flags and signs are very telling. He only uses women for what he can get out of them before he discards them. What he really desires is a man. You can thank his mama for beating him to death and neglecting him.

His mother never taught her son how to properly love and respect women at all. A Narcissistic mother tends to baby her son while abusing him and grooming him to take on the husband role in her life. In the event that she should ever end up single and lonely, she can call on her son-husband to fulfill her needs. This woman is dangerous. She will allow her son to do whatever he wants to keep him coming back to her. This ensures her that the umbilical cord will stay intact. She thinks her son is her soul mate instead of her actual child.

If a man happens to bring home a new girlfriend and introduces her to his toxic mother, she will hate his new woman. Mama feels as if she is entitled to have her son's heart, not you. Sad to say this, but mom will always assist her son with sabotaging **ALL** of his relationships. She will always inadvertently try to control her son's love life by interjecting her toxic presence and playing on his weaknesses. He can never deny his mother the attention she craves, and she will use this to her advantage. I've even seen a woman "pretend" to be sick in the emergency room just to pull her son away from his girlfriend. Where do you think her son learned how to manipulate women? He learned this behavior from his Narcissistic Mommy!

That's why he gets into continuous fights with the women he dates, because when he argues, subconsciously he thinks he's really fighting with his mother. He takes his anger and rage that he feels for his mother, out on his current girlfriend. He can't subconsciously separate his mama from his girlfriend. He doesn't know how. When he feels resentment towards you, he really is feeling resentment towards his mother. He hates all women because he hates her. She ruined him.

She will vicariously abuse you through her son. She will act as if she adores her new "daughter-in-law" but she will secretly plot to help her son cheat and lie to you. She assists him with destroying all of his relationships so that he can go running back to her

to vent about his problems to keep him close to her.

Stay away from both of them. It's a no win

situation and she's not gonna let you have her son.

Narcissistic Supply

Okay ladies, so you go through his phone while he's sleeping (bad, bad girl) and you see a plethora of text messages from various numbers. You open up his text message thread and see a picture of the woman he's been gallivanting around town behind your back. She's the complete opposite of you: short, stubby, acne, fake gaudy jewelry, loud, ratchet and much younger than your ex (in other words, she's a naïve airhead). Here you are, tall, curvaceous, beautiful, educated, accomplished, self-sufficient, church-going, good credit, great job and you volunteer at a weekly soup kitchen. You're a great catch and more than a man could ask for. You love, support and give your man anything he wants and you replenish all of his needs. The sex has never been better (as he claims he wants it all of the time). You cook his hot meals with love. You surprise him with little gifts of affection. He asks you to support his new business venture by lending him money to launch his company, (unfortunately, he can't turn to his trifling friends and family members for financial help) and you gladly oblige because you're his #1 supporter. You are his "rock" and then some. So can somebody please answer this million dollar question? Why does he cheat when he's receiving everything a man could ever want and need from a woman? Why does he cheat on you with a downgrade?

The answer is simple. He cheats on you because (#1) He can easily control her knowing she has low self-esteem; she will believe all of his lies without first investigating his relationship status. She makes him feel superior because he's incredibly insecure when he's standing next to you. He secretly envies you and your ambition, so he needs someone who is easier to manipulate when you're not around. (#2) She is willing to sleep with him right away, so he can squeeze her in while you're at work or out grocery shopping. (#3) The trifling bitch has no self-respect for herself nor does she care that she's fucking someone else's man. She doesn't have an ounce of integrity (hell, she may even be a Narcissist herself) and she's not going to leave him alone. She figures that settling for a piece of a man is better than not having a man at all. In her mind, she feels validated for fuckin up someone else's relationship.

Hello, meet the side chick/ downgrade/ hood rat. But on a serious note, your Narcissistic ex doesn't view his side piece (better known as your replacement) as a human being, he only identifies her as a sexual object. Matter of fact, he views EVERYONE as mere objects who all have the ability to provide him with different levels of attention and adulation. Any type of attention from anyone is considered **Narcissistic supply**.

His circle of friends provide him with Narcissistic supply (*attention, admiration, adulation*). His family provides him with Narcissistic supply (*love, support, forgiveness*). His circle of rotated sexual partners provides him with Narcissistic supply (*sex, ego-stroking, food, money*). The Narcissist cannot survive without his supply. He has to lie and manipulate people on a consistent basis in order to maintain his supply it at all times. Sustaining Narcissistic supply is a matter of life and death to a Narcissist. He feels validated as long as he's pulling the puppet strings. He feels very powerful knowing he's lying, manipulating and controlling people. **Attention and Adulation = Narcissistic Supply**. That's right, <u>**ANY**</u> kind of attention, whether it's good or bad attention, is considered **NARCISSISTIC SUPPLY**.

Whether you're cussing him out or flirting with him, it's all considered "supply," so please don't give him any. If he wants supply, let him get it from his harem of rotated sex partners or his circle of toxic friends. Got it? Good.

Four Phases of Narcissistic Abuse

There is a cycle of abuse that the Narcissist adheres to when he initiates a new romantic relationship. It's unfortunate that you were targeted to be added to that list, but at least you are now aware of your ex's bullshit tactics so that you can prevent it from happening to you all over again. There are four phases that you will undergo when you are involved with a Narcissist:

Love-Bombing Phase

This is the initial period where the Narcissist pursues you and pours on the compliments extra heavy. He suddenly is interested in all of your hobbies. He takes you to meet his friends and family (Newsflash: everyone you meet from his inner circle are in on the scheme to help him score and seduce you. Trust me, they've met many other women before you). He wines and dines you. He makes you feel like you're floating on cloud nine. He's figuring out your weak spots so that he can sink his teeth into you later for the kill.

He will "mirror" your qualities and morph into everything you ever wanted in a man. The Narcissist has no identity. He is empty and he has to emulate your good qualities to make you fall in love with him. Your ex is a chameleon. He has repeated this cycle with hundreds of women before you. He has the game perfected. He has aggressively studied you and learned your strengths, your weaknesses, your flaws, your achievements, your insecurities and everything else that makes you special. With all of this information, he will create a personalized blue print to take over your life and destroy you after he's done using you. The very same thing that he loves about you, will be the very same thing that he hates about you. The reality is, he never loved you in the first place. It's a hard pill to swallow, but don't feel bad, he doesn't love himself either. He loves control. That's all and that's it.

Idealization Phase

The second stage of abuse is idealization. During this time, he has gotten you to drop your defenses. You're an open book. You're in love with him and it happened all too fast. You're usually too smart to allow yourself to fall so hard and so fast for a man, but it's too late, you've already let this man "woo" you over. This is what Narcissists do best and they do it well. No matter how educated or intelligent you are, the Narcissist will find a way to get into your mind as well as your heart. Right now, he is giving you endless sex and courting you while secretly trying to figure out where you keep your credit cards stashed and what other types of perks he can collect from you. Oh baby, he is plotting and planning your demise as he kisses you softly on the lips; the whole time you're blinded by what you deem is love. The Narcissist is a magician and your relationship is an illusion constructed on his terms in order to control you. He wants to claim credit for all of **YOUR** hard work. He wants your identity, your nice car, your connections and your status. He wants to eat your food, use your credit cards and cheat on you to keep you stressed out and walking on eggshells. His tactics are well- calculated.

The Narcissist isn't in love with you. He never was. He's great at pretending that he is in love (he's had quite a lot of practice). He will pretend to love your friends, your children and your family. His goal is to slowly isolate you away from your loved ones so that they won't suspect him of any abuse. While you're falling head over heels in love with him, he's carefully plotting to sleep with other women behind your back because he has you right where he wants you. He can only keep up with the fake facade but for so long. He is a great actor. Enjoy it while you can because it won't last for long. He's now preparing to pull the rug from under your feet. You're in for a real emotional rollercoaster, so strap on your seat belt and hold on tight.

Devalue Phase

Suddenly you notice a change in his behavior. He blows hot and cold. The man who once told you he worshipped the ground you walked on, is now acting aloof, lying and pulling disappearing acts.

He initiates a manipulation tactic called "gas lighting" where he will constantly play mind games to mess with your head. He will tell you the sky is red and you'll look up and see that the sky is actually blue. You'll begin to question yourself and doubt that the sky is actually blue. Your ex uses this tactic whenever you suspect him of cheating. If you see him talking or flirting with another female, he will lie about it directly to your face. He can kiss the girl on the lips and convince you that the kiss wasn't what it appeared to be. You can walk in on him having sex and he will convince you that the woman he's screwing means nothing to him and he was only "dry humping" her. You can find condoms in his car with his semen in it, and he will still deny it. The Narcissist gets off on watching you try to piece together his lies and foolery. He loves to see you squirm with fury and confusion. Discombobulation is the name of the Narcissist's deadly game. He wants to keep you off balance as much as possible in order to maintain the upper hand. He's conditioned you to accept his abuse and you will begin to feel like there's no way to escape his evil grasp.

As he devalues you, he is also sleeping with his next victim behind your back. He is grooming her and love bombing her in preparation for your departure. He's planning your exit and you don't even know it. He doesn't like the fact that you're beginning to question his actions and his outright blatant disrespect. He doesn't care that you've noticed a change in his behavior. He does what he wants when he wants. His mama allows him to be disrespectful, so you're not going to come along switching shit up now! How dare you?

The Narcissist begins to spew his anger and insecurities at you. He accuses you of cheating (*when he's really the one cheating*). He starts to tell you how miserable he is with you, but he's not ready to break up with you yet. He will downplay your achievements and accolades. He cannot hide his hidden jealousy and hostility towards you anymore. He loathes you and holds you in contempt for loving him despite him disrespecting you all of the time.

"*Projection*" is when he accuses you of the things he really feels about himself or either the dishonorable cheating that he's doing when you're not around. If he calls you ugly, then he's really

talking about himself, but projecting it onto you.
He feels ugly about himself, so he wants you to feel
the same. If he says you will never find a man to
marry you, what he's really saying is that he won't
be able to find anyone on your level to marry him in
the future because he knows he's a shitty, toxic
abuser. He may marry a thot, but he's not gonna
land a top notch chick like you to walk down that
aisle with him. He's secretly hoping that you won't
find a man better than him and get married.

The Narcissist is excellent at projecting his
insecurities and deep-rooted issues onto you. He
will never hold himself accountable when the
relationship is falling apart. He wants you to know
that it's all of your fault and there's nothing you can
do to fix it. If you complain, he will punish you by
disappearing (ghosting). He wants to train you to

accept his whorish ways. You better take the little bit of community dick he's offering or else he will give it to his new bitch to make you suffer. You're NOT supposed to question him in the first place. He feels entitled to treat you this way and he will torture you if you go against him. He figures that this is what you signed up for, so he wants you to shut the hell up or suffer the consequences.

Discard Phase

The Narcissist has blatantly disrespected you one time too many. At this point, he is screwing multiple women and he could care less if it hurts you. He doesn't care that you see women calling and texting his phone. He's constantly belittling you and telling you how miserable he is in the relationship, yet he doesn't want you to move on. He still wants to use you for money, sex and anything else he can get out of you while he's

fucking his new victim behind your back. He

doesn't care. He doesn't respect you. The

relationship meant nothing to him. He's bored and

rather hang with his boys (he may even be fucking

his boys on the low too). He wants you to know

that he rather be anywhere else besides being with

you. He hates you and makes it his business to let

you know every chance he gets. He's told all of his

friends that he is no longer with you. He's smeared

you to his mama and his friends after all that you

have done for him. You've remained faithful and

loyal, so what the fuck is his problem? Why is he

sabotaging a relationship that he begged you for

when he first pursued the fuck out of you?

He is a motherfucking monster, full of deceit and

immoral principles. He is a disloyal backstabber,

storyteller and shit talker. Welcome to the world of demonic possession. No one with integrity behaves like this towards people. However, the Narcissist does. You have to understand that the Narcissist has no remorse, no empathy or intellectual communication skills. Your ex doesn't have the mental or emotional capacity to have an in-depth conversation to resolve interpersonal problems. He's childish and shallow. Narcissists never compromise.

The Narcissist has a maladaptive character disorder. Don't try to understand it. Just run like hell once he's exposed his true self to you because the only cure for him is death. You won't win if you stick around. You have been discarded. If you're smart enough, you will have discarded the Narcissist first before he does it to you. Consider the cheating, lies and betrayal as a blessing. If you go back to him, you can expect more abusive behavior because he thinks you actually enjoy it. If you cheat on him to get back at him, he will just compete with you and fuck more bitches and throw it in your face. He lives for the drama!

He now considers you as a damaged possession that he can store on his shelf until he's ready to return to abuse it some more. One venomous conquest after the next, the Narcissist will purposely sabotage all of his relationships. He has a permanent dark cloud floating above him and it follows him around everywhere he goes. His karma will always be bad and he is willing to share his negative energy with his victims.

Ghosting

Ghosting is a very popular term that is used mostly in reference to short-term relationships. People are known to "ghost" when they are actively dating and soon find out that they aren't compatible with their potential mate. It's a cowardly but easy way to ditch their newfound prospect. Men are also known to ghost after they've had a sexual encounter. Their sole purpose is to get into your panties without the hassle of being in a committed relationship. Once you've accepted his terms, you grant him permission to sleep with you and abandon you. No explanation is owed to you for his exit. All he cares about is sleeping with you. You've allowed him to dictate the terms of your "situationship" and you cannot question him about it, when he decides to ghost on you. You either keep fucking him or ditch him and move on.

In the case of the Narcissist, he will ghost on you in the midst of his committed relationship. He doesn't have the ability to work through any relationship obstacles with you. He rather ghost and fuck bitches behind your back to escape accountability. He cannot have a mature conversation with you to work towards a compromise when a problem arises. He rather bail out on you and chill with his boys. He will do something disrespectful or hurtful knowing you don't like it, however, he will ghost to avoid the consequences once you confront him about it. A Narcissist will abuse this ghosting tactic as long as you allow him to.

The sick thing about ghosting is that while he's out busy entertaining other women or kicking with his boys, he's also training you to accept his disappearing acts. He will punish you by ghosting if you hold him accountable for being disrespectful. He will return when he feels he's made you suffer enough. See, he doesn't want to be held accountable for his disrespectful behavior. He doesn't want to work out any problems between you two unless there is an incentive or perk involved. He prefers friction and drama. He wants to keep you paranoid and on your toes at all hours of the night. You have been molded into his personal flunky to accept the crumbs and table scraps. If you complain about anything, he will train you to keep your opinions and grievances to yourself or you will run the risk of losing him for a couple of days or even weeks. He gets the pleasure of leaving you unhinged while he's off enjoying his day and he gets to enjoy the benefits of returning to you with your arms wide open, waiting to submit and serve him. If you don't comply, he will disappear again and stay away longer. Peep game.

Ghosting is a manipulation tactic to get you to chase or submit to your Narcissist. It's his way of running the relationship his way and making you suffer for calling him out on his disrespectful behavior. He wants you to chase him when he ghosts, beg him to come home and silence your complaints. It's all about submission and control. His mama don't question him or his whereabouts, so you're not going to do it to him either. He oversteps his boundaries with everyone and doesn't answer to no one. Not even his mother. He controls the ebb and the flow of the relationship, not you. You better fall in line. This is not normal in any relationship.

If your partner is making you run behind him like a dog chasing a cat, then it's time for you to re-think this relationship through. Start planning your exit strategy NOW. If you live together, then you need to start searching for a new place to live even if it means moving in with a friend or family member. Pack your bags, shut off any utilities in your name and ghost on him before he returns. Relationships should not consist of mind games and manipulation tactics. If he's too immature to sit down and hash out problems like a real man, then he doesn't need to be in a relationship at all. Do yourself a favor by removing yourself from his circus. Let him be a clown for the next chick. You need a real man who can communicate and be a good listener and problem solver. Leave your Narcissistic ex alone. His mother obviously didn't teach him how to respectfully communicate with a woman because she is the only one dumb enough to tolerate his childish bullshit and that's exactly how she wants it. She loves her abusive, codependent relationship with her toxic son. You have better things to do with your time. Stop allowing him to waste yours. Time is money and you can't get any of that time back. Just chuck it up as a bad investment and move on.

Listen, the right guy won't run when relationship challenges arise, but a fuck boy will. Reclaim your time and let that grown boy go!

No Contact

This is the hard part. The deafening silence. The mourning of what you thought was a loving relationship. The grieving over a man who was nothing more than a distorted illusion. You're left with the memories and the pain of trying to piece together the confusion of the betrayal and deception. You want answers. You need to know why has your ex-boyfriend come into your life just to destroy you. Unfortunately, the Narcissist will never give you that closure. This is when you have to find your own closure by going **NO CONTACT**.

Block him for life. He's toxic for your soul and poisonous for your spirit. The relationship is over. The reality has set in that you don't have access to his to his life anymore. You are no longer hanging out at the places you and him use to frequent (or at least you shouldn't be). It's over. Just like that, all of the beautiful memories you both shared are gone. The holidays you spent together are dark reminders of yesteryear. The vacations you enjoyed together mean nothing. It's all a distant memory. This is the hard part. Forcing yourself to pretend that your ex doesn't exist. This means no texting. No phone calls. No emails. No third party contact. Nothing. The relationship will never be the same if you do decide to take him back. He will continue to abuse you more if you let him back in. He's severely disordered and cannot bring himself to change for the better.

Now chances are that you will be tempted to contact your ex one last time just to vent to him. After all, he did cheat and emotionally scar you. It's not something that anyone with a heart can easily get over. However, going strict **no contact** requires great restraint. I will be honest, I broke contact on multiple occasions just to let my ex know that he was a walking STD with no ambition to improve his life as a 40+ year old man. I had so much pinned up anger and frustration towards him. I have no regrets for cussing him out. By the end of our relationship, he had done so many abusive and cruel things to me. I didn't care. He was a bully who physically assaulted me, used up my finances, gossiped behind my back and cheated every chance he could get. My anger was justified. I could care less if he told everyone I was crazy. Anyone with common sense knows that if you toy with someone's emotions and destroy their hopes of love, then that said person has every right to be full of rage and anger (just be responsible enough to avoid doing something illegal like destroying his car or busting out his windows; he's not worth the jail time).

There will be small issues that arise after the break up. Your ex will either have left some of his belongings at your place or you will have left your things at his place. If he's a true Narcissist, he will use his belongings as leverage to keep a foot in the door to keep communicating with you. Or he will either hold on to your belongings to keep you running behind him. I've been there and done that. My best advice is to let your ex keep your shit. Consider your belongings gone. If he has a set of your house keys or car keys, let him have it. Take it as a loss and pay the extra money to have your locks changed. Leave his sorry ass in the past. A decent man would return your property without the bullshit games, but a Narcissist will hold on to your shit to keep you stringing along because he needs your constant attention after the relationship has ended. He feels validated knowing he can dangle your possessions in your face just to keep you running behind him. Let him have that shit. Material things can be replaced. Cut your losses and apply the lesson accordingly. Your future husband should be the only man with access to your car and your apartment. Stop giving husband privileges to a boyfriend. He hasn't earned it!

If he has left his belongings at your place, send him an email requesting him to pick up his belongings within the next seven days. Let him know in the email that if he does not pick up his items by the requested deadline, that you will dispose of his shit in the trash. Print a copy of the email and mail it to his home address via certified mail. Save all of your receipts because if you end up putting his shit on the curb and he tries to take you to small claims court in the future, you will have evidence to show to the judge that you gave the bastard a chance to obtain his belongings, but he never came to pick up his trash. Cover your tail at all times when dealing with the Narcissist.

No contact is critical to your healing process. If you continue to break contact, you will delay your recovery time for your healing. You will continue to repeat what you refuse to repair and you won't see any results until you put in the work to stay **no contact**. Deactivate your Facebook page, go into hiatus and do what you need to do to stay off of your ex's radar until you're feeling better. During this time, you should be self-reflecting and seeking therapy to repair your self-esteem. **No contact** is the only way you can move on from a Narcissist. He won't change. Not now. Not even ten or twenty years from now. You, however, do have the power to change for the better. Stop procrastinating and start taking baby steps towards your healing.

Hoovering

So you've caught him cheating and you already did the inevitable by breaking up with him (if he hasn't discarded you first). What's next? Well in true Narcissistic fashion, your ex is NOT finished with you. He has to make sure that you're grieving and broken after he has moved on to his new victim. He should be focused on building a new beginning with the new chick right? I mean after all, he's rubbing his latest "situationship" in your face. He wants you to believe that he's found his long lost love in this new woman of his. He wants to make sure that you see how happy he is now and that you were the cause of his infidelity issues throughout the relationship. He wants you to feel that your nagging him is the real reason he cheated on you. It's all of your fault. Now he's going to torture you by showing the world how happy he is with the woman he cheated on you with. He's going to pour salt into your wounds to make your heart sting.

The only problem is this: if he's so happy with her, then why is he so focused on stalking and harassing you? Why is he going so hard to prove to you that he is happier with her? Why isn't his energy invested into building a healthy future with his new bitch? Why does he want to prevent you from moving on? Why is he trying to suck you back in after he's made it clear that he doesn't want to be in a relationship with you anymore? He can't be all that happy with her when he's too busy focusing on you.

The term "Hoovering" comes from the Hoover vacuum cleaner. Whenever your ex-boyfriend focuses on trying to pull you back into the old relationship, he's deliberately preventing you from moving on. He wants to "suck" you back into his web of lies and confusion while he parades his new chick around town. This is called **Hoovering** (just like the vacuum cleaner). He's sucking you back into his world. You're not allowed to move on, but he is. You're not allowed to heal or date new people, but he is. You're not allowed to have a new life outside of his life. As far as he's concerned, he is your life. You better not replace him with a new guy. He wants to maintain control over your life, even after he has jumped into some new pussy. He will tell his friends and family that he doesn't care about you anymore, but the whole time, he is low-key stalking you and watching your every move; waiting for you to grow weak in hopes that you allow him to come back. He wants to fuck up your life some more. He is sadistic and enjoys watching you grieve and squirm over him. In all actuality, he's not worth the gum stuck on the bottom of your shoe. Dodge the hoover maneuver and focus on becoming successful.

Hoovering is a malicious control tactic. The Narcissist is deeply insecure and has to maintain ties to all of his ex-girlfriends. I don't care how long ago he dated his old chicks. Ten years, twenty years, last year. He is going to stalk **ALL** of his exes. The only way he can feel validated is through control. If he can keep tabs on all of his ex-girlfriends, he will feel powerful and self-entitled. He will continue to pry and wait for you to fall vulnerable while he rotates his low grade sexual partners. He will hoover you and he will hoover her. He will hoover all of his exes. He doesn't want you to move on. Not now. Not ever. He leads a pathetic, empty life and he needs your validation. He will send people to contact you in the event that you make his pursuit difficult (flying monkeys). If you disappear from social media and move far away out of his sight, he will have his toxic flying monkey friends reach out and message you through text or inbox messages. He will use mutual friends on Facebook to stalk you and reel you back in. He will create fake pages and try to send you friend requests in hopes that he can connect and spy on your Facebook page. He will call your family members and ask about you. He is obsessed and forever will be. The entire time, he's fucking multiple (men and women) and spreading his community dick all around town.

The best thing you can do at this point is to ignore all of his Hoovering attempts. If your mutual friends persist in sending messages from him after you have warned them all to stop, then you must block them at all costs. Change your phone number if you need to. Move to a new city or state if it helps to re-shift your focus. Get the fuck out of dodge for a while because he's going to stalk you forever. The Hoovering is set up to rattle your nerves, create anxiety and induce paranoia. The Narcissist doesn't want you to live in peace because he's not a peaceful person. He knows deep down inside that if you escape his grasp and begin to heal, then you will get your life back on track without him in the picture. He doesn't want you to bounce back and become successful. He knows that success is the greatest revenge and it will burn him inside to see you level up bigger and better than you ever have before.

Word to the wise, please reject his Hoovering attempts. He's not going to change. He hasn't had an epiphany all of a sudden. He's actually going to repeat the same cycle with his new chick and the chick after her. She just doesn't know it yet. Wash, rinse and repeat.

Go and build a new life for yourself and allow God to turn your mess into a "message." Know that God will use your last relationship as an escape to a door leading you to a lifetime of prosperity. Position yourself to receive an abundance of blessings. God doesn't bless mess honey, so don't go back to your ex. Just say no to Hoovering!

Flying Monkeys: Abuse by Proxy

When I was a little girl, I remember watching the movie classic, "The Wizard of Oz" for the very first time. The villain in the film happened to be the evil Wicked Witch of the West. She was one scary, green-faced antagonist with a vindictive agenda to hunt down poor Dorothy. The Wicked Witch of the West envied Dorothy because she possessed a pair of ruby red slippers once owned by her sister, the Wicked Witch of the East. When she failed to get the ruby slippers off of Dorothy's feet at the behest of her deceased sister, the vile witch had to retreat back to her dark castle to come up with another plan to retrieve the shoes. The witch decided to send her troupe of flying monkeys to capture Dorothy to bring her back to her headquarters. The villainess orchestrated a plan to capture Dorothy without getting her hands dirty. She sent her ugly minions. Let me introduce to you the **flying monkey**.

The Narcissist's inner circle of friends, family members as well as his harem of sexual partners are considered to be his "Flying Monkeys" (enablers of *his* toxic abuse). Your ex's inner circle will ALWAYS side with him no matter how guilty he is. If he cheats on you and/or abuses you, his **flying monkeys** will cover for him. If he assaults you or degrades you, his friends will look the other way. They know his true character because their character is toxic as well. His flying monkey friends will ALWAYS give him a pass to do "fuck boy" shit because nine times out of ten, they're all fuck boys and fuck girls too! Birds of feather flock together. Seriously, what type of friend with integrity would enable another friend to abuse a human being like this? If you have anyone in your inner circle who enjoys inflicting abuse upon innocent people, then you may have to reevaluate their purpose in your life. If you see nothing wrong with associating with a toxic person, then perhaps you're a Narcissist too. The Narcissist's friends are not his real friends. They are enablers of *his* abuse. They can't be trusted nor should you communicate with them at all. They are nothing more than an extension of your Narcissistic ex.

A Flying Monkey is simply a weak-minded messenger, stalker, minion and pawn. An invalidated servant with low self-esteem whom the Narcissist can use to do his bidding in order to keep his hands squeaky clean from all accusations of stalking. After you break up with the Narcissist, he will try to send one of his flying monkeys to communicate with you to prevent you from moving on. His minions will reject any evidence you present against the Narcissist to prove he abused you. Their #1 goal is to carry out the Narcissist's orders. They will sit up and gossip with you negatively about the Narcissist and take back the information to the Narcissist. They play both sides of the fence to keep the drama going on behalf of your ex. The Narcissist is a great story teller and he will tell everyone that you're the bad guy just to get people to side with him. He seeks out weak people who are just as Narcissistic and toxic as he is, to deliver the messages to you. You're not allowed to move on from the break up and the flying monkeys will ensure that you have a hard time doing so. Their loyalty is to the Narcissist. Yes, this is considered stalking and harassment. The flying monkey seeks validation from the Narcissist by working as his assailant. They are sadists as well.

These people are fucking miserable! Who has time to run a smear campaign against someone they don't know outside of what your Narcissistic ex tells them? How can anyone speak about your character when they don't know you? The sad thing about Flying Monkeys is that they will gossip about anyone without having their facts straight just because their Narcissistic friend (your ex) started the rumor. They are nothing but toxic enablers!

So please be wary of anyone passing messages to you from your ex. Please block all mutual friends on Facebook. No, you don't need to be Facebook friends with any of his family either. Trust me, they are watching you and taking back information to your ex as well. Shut all of that down. No more middle men or problematic messengers. You have to establish boundaries and keep toxic people out of your personal space. Anyone that is connected to your ex must be blocked. No ifs, ands or buts about it! Protect your energy and stay toxic free. Your ex has an agenda to ruin your life because you won't go back to him. Avoid his circle of friends and family at all costs. They ride for him no matter how much of a good woman you were to him. Don't forget that.

The Smear Campaign

A man will do one of two things after he's lost a good woman: #1. He will cry in silence, learn the lesson and do better with his next relationship. He will grow from his past experiences and mature in preparation for the new love in his life. #2. Or he will become a "Bitter Bob" and run a treacherous smear campaign about you to prevent other people from liking you. In the Narcissist's case, if you are a quality woman and you treated him like a king during your relationship, he's going to run a malicious smear campaign full of lies and vicious rumors to completely destroy your reputation. You escaped the relationship and he fears that people will find out that he's the real abuser. So in return, he has to do serious damage control and perception management to destroy your credibility. He gossips and smears your name in order to get the negative focus off of him.

Smear campaigns can get real messy after a break up. I've been the subject of one and they're really stressful to deal with. Your ex will have all types of strangers believing his bullshit rhetoric about you. He will even reach out to your family and close friends to cry victim and paint you out to be the bad guy. He discusses every private detail of your relationship, but he will add his own little twist of lies and fabrications to make the story even juicier. He's suffering internally and his ego has taken a major blow. He now feels that he has to run a pathetic smear campaign because the last thing he needs is people talking about him like a dog. The truth would expose him and force him into hiding. The damage to his ego would traumatize him.

Remember that he has to maintain control of everything in his life. His insecurities won't allow for accountability of his wrongdoings. He will smear and destroy you before you get a chance to do it to him. He has to maintain the control of the ebb and flow of the relationship at all times, even after it is long over.

I'm sorry that he has done this to you. He's immature and he can't help himself. He has a permanent character disorder. Narcissists are nothing more than toddlers trapped inside of adult bodies. They cannot think or comprehend past a surface level. Mature adults do not have to resort to such childish tactics. When a relationship is over, you move on. It takes too much energy to try to destroy your ex's reputation. You're not getting paid to do it, so why bother?

If you happen to be caught in the middle of an ugly smear campaign, do your best to ignore it and maintain your boundaries. Ignore, ignore, ignore! The rumors will eventually stop and people won't care in the long run. The only people that entertain smear campaigns are your ex's toxic inner circle of fake friends. Anyone with a discerning spirit, would be hesitant to repeat gossip about someone they don't know personally. The Narcissist will always make sure that he is surrounded by people who enable his bullshit and toxicity. Rise above it and stay on the path to success. Soon enough, you'll be so far past your ex and his flying monkey friends, that they will be embarrassed for spreading rumors about you in the first place. If God is showering you with new blessings, how will your ex and his friends look when their rumors start to backfire? This is how a smear campaign works to your advantage. Their lies about you will have them looking like idiots who lack good moral judgment. Trust me, your ex's friends and family know that you were a good woman to him, so they should all be ashamed of themselves for helping him run a smear campaign against you. Like I said, please continue to shine. You will eventually laugh at this drama in the end. They will all wish that they would have treated you better once God starts blessing you in their face! Karma is a bitch.

Triangulation

There are two types of women that your ex will jump into a new relationship with:

Woman #1: The spiritually and morally good girl who has the same, similar characteristics as you do (that's why he targeted her). She's a good woman who got caught up with your lying, cheating ex. He started seeing her while he was still in a relationship with you. He didn't inform her that he already had a special lady in his life. She was blindsided and just as shocked when she found out about you. She's not an evil woman seeking to destroy you. Her heart is pure and she's trying to make sense of the cheating just as you once were. When he starts to treat her bad, she will do her own detective work and find out about his other women. If she finds your number or your Facebook profile, she *may*

contact you out of curiosity. Don't be mean to her.
Be cordial, but frank. Give her some good advice
and keep it stepping. Stay out of it and let her work
it out on her own. You don't owe her any
explanation for your ex's bad behavior. She has to
learn the hard way just as you did. Pray for her.
She will need the strength to fight the ugly spiritual
battle that awaits her after the breakup. He's doing
to her what he already has done to you: *sadistic
abuse and serial cheating.*

Woman #2: The trifling hood rat who is just as
toxic and Narcissistic as your ex. She enjoys
stalking and harassing you. She enjoys taunting
you and rubbing her new relationship in your face.
She constantly brings your name up and gossips
about you to her friends. Her obsession with you is
an understatement. She is willing to stalk you and

report back to your ex on what she saw you doing just to prove her loyalty to him. She is a willing and able minion of your ex. Her self-esteem is so low, she will allow your ex to use her as his personal tool, to intrude on your life. She knows your ex secretly is in love with you, because he won't stop talking about you. Unfortunately, she needs that validation from him, even if it means stalking and harassing you on his behalf. There's a good chance that she may be a Narcissist herself. Sounds dysfunctional? Well it is. How can two people claim to be happy and in a healthy relationship, when they are both teaming up to destroy your life? Welp, this is the life of a Narcissist. And hell no, he's not going to change for her either. Let it all play out because the deception coming her way will be unwarranted and severe. He's using her to hurt you for moving on from him after you caught him cheating with *her*. The nerve right? When you stop reacting to him and her, he will get mad and take his frustrations out on her, then ghost on her to seek out another sexual partner to groom all over again. She is of no use to him anymore because he can't get you to react to his trouble-making concubine. He is using the poor girl to bait you in order to keep you entangled with him and on your mind. He also wants you to believe that he is being sought after and desired by other women. This is called "Triangulation." A dirty manipulation tactic to make you feel jealous, insecure and make you want to compete against the other woman for your ex's attention again. The mind games are stupid and endless with a Narcissist.

Triangulation is a strategy used by the Narcissist to create rivalry and drama between his new lover and his ex-lover. The Narcissist will gossip to his new chick by filling her head with lies about all of the horrible things you did to him. His fabricated stories will have you looking like an obsessed stalker who can't seem to get over him. After he finishes running his big, lying mouth, he will then have his delusional side chick contact you in order to harass you further. He gets to sit back and watch two women argue over him. His agenda is to make himself appear desirable to his ex and at the same time, keep his new woman on her toes by making her compete against his ex. In his mind, he really hopes that this tactic will make you want him back because he wants you to feel as if his new bitch won the prize that you lost. You have to laugh at this fuckery. He can't be serious right? Are we in high school or are we adults? Two words: boy bye.

Why do Narcissists triangulate? Well, I can tell you that if you are wise to his game playing, then you won't fall for this old mind trick. He wants you to believe that he has dozens of women lined up ready to fight over him. That's not the case. It's a sneaky plot and desperate attempt to get you to chase after him again. He wants to continue to emotionally torment you because you're NOT running behind him as he hoped you would when he discarded the relationship. He knows that his new "*fool of a woman*" will jump through fiery hoops because she seeks his validation. He can't understand why you are not doing the same (it's because you respect yourself enough to not chase behind a bum ass low life who needs to cheat in order to feel like a man).

So he resorts to connecting you both through a silly 3-way argument. Click bait.

If you find yourself at the brunt of a messy Narcissistic love triangle, please don't engage in arguing with his new dummy. It's a set up. He has already smeared you badly to her and she thinks you're crazy. She has yet to find out that she's next in line to be cheated on and toyed with. Ignore the bait and allow her to find out on her own. He will soon triangulate his new chick with the woman he plans to cheat on her with. The Narcissist repeats this cycle with every woman he's involved with, trust me. In order to make himself feel validated, he has to arrange a catfight between his new girl and his old flame. Only weak men do shit like that. If he was so happy with his new chick, he wouldn't even focus on hurting his ex. Please don't entertain this bullshit. Walk away and ignore both of them. She's not on your level anyway and never will be. I mean, what type of woman would gloat over someone else's "sloppy seconds" just to rub it in your face? It says a lot about her character right? Don't worry, she's got hers coming too. He's grooming her the same way he groomed you when he first fell in love with you. The difference between you and her is that she's easier to *"train"* like a dog because she suffers from an extreme case of low self-esteem. Your ex had to work hard to get you, but with this new chick, he basically can toss her a few compliments and he's got her chasing him like a puppy. The older the Narcissist gets, the younger and dumber his new girlfriends become. The Narcissist wants the new girl as gullible and naïve as possible. It makes his job easy when she doesn't value herself. It's really pathetic that she thinks you're mad that she won the plastic toy in the bottom of the Cracker Jack box. Oh really? Ha!

Why should you be mad for? You've already slept with the man Lord knows how many times and you put up with his shit. You've been there and done that. No woman can ever make you jealous over a man with dirty poverty penis. Especially if he's broke and abusive. Why would you feel threatened because she's enjoying your "sloppy seconds?" Seriously, she has no idea that you're relieved that she took out the trash for you and is now the target of his chronic cheating and deception. He is now **HER** problem. He will destroy her life if not worse. Fall back, get your popcorn and tea ready because the Narc's reality show is coming.

The Narcissist's Facebook Harem

Social media makes it incredibly easy for a weak-minded man to cheat on his significant other. The Narcissist is able to maintain a digital rolodex of booty calls via his inbox. Technology has made it far too accessible for any serial cheater to sustain multiple romantic relationships online.

Facebook, a popular social media platform, is the Narcissist's favorite predatory playground for finding new pussy. The majority of his Facebook friends on his friend's list are comprised of old fuck buddies, ex-girlfriends with poor self-esteem, high school sweethearts, crazy ex-stalkers and sister wives. If you're not a Facebook friend of your Narcissist ex, then pat yourself on the back. It only means that you know your value and you have no desire to be Facebook friends with him. You refuse to have any affiliations with your ex because he mistreated you and he did not appreciate you when he had you. And for that, you will not allow yourself to bless his presence ever again, not even as a Facebook friend because you prioritize your self-worth above anything else. But what about all of the other women who choose to stay connected to your ex? They obviously have self-esteem issues. Say hello to the Narcissist's Harem. **There is endless Narcissistic supply hiding all throughout your ex's social media!**

Your ex's harem is nothing more than a collection of old, used up toys (women) that have collected dust and are awaiting to be used again. The Narcissist will store his old toys on a shelf and leave all of them lonely and destitute until he's ready to circle back and play with them again. His "toys" are there to validate his existence when he's in-between Grade A supply relationships. They are all sources of low grade supply and will serve a specific purpose when the Narcissist summons any one of them.

For instance, your ex may call on one of his former chicks from his harem and use her to spy on you and your whereabouts on his behalf. She will then take this information that she has obtained from watching you and relay it back to him. He will recruit her to become a flying monkey for the sole purpose of haunting you and harassing you. Each female from the Narcissist's harem, benefits him in one way or another. Whether he needs a quick roll in the hay or a monetary favor or a cooked meal, he can call one of his wenches from his harem and they will come a 'running! Don't be _**THAT**_ girl!

Future-Faking

Lies, lies and more lies! Whenever the Narcissist's lips are moving, just know that he's *always* lying! If you have allowed him the privilege of hoovering you back into the relationship, you will find it hard to resist. This is because he promises you that he will change for the better knowing damn well he's not going to follow through on any of his promises. At this point, you should be ignoring his lying ass, but the temptation is just too strong. The soul tie is wrapped around you tight and the trauma bond is breaking you down. You're too weak to stand your ground and you end up responding to his text messages. He knows just what to say to get you to cave in and drop your defenses. He promises you that he will never cheat on you again. He promises to give you a big diamond ring. He promises you a big wedding. He promises you he will buy you a dream house with a white picket fence. He promises to fly you to Paris. Girlfriend, I've got some news for you, [**don't hold your breath**] these promises will never be fulfilled!

He will say anything at this point to get you to come back to him in order to repeat the cycle of abuse to punish you for leaving him. This is also known as **"Future-Faking."**

I really don't understand how some women can continue to believe the endless lies time after time, again and again. One time is one time too many. If he really loved you, he would never put himself in a position to lose you. A real man doesn't talk the talk, but he makes it his business to "*show*" you that he will walk the walk (*you're so worth it*).

A real man has integrity. He knows your worth and he knows you're one of a kind. He's not going to jeopardize his relationship and risk losing you to the next man. Only a sucker would pull a stunt like this to try to slither his way back into your life. Why do you continue to allow this creep to fill your head up with empty promises? You deserve so much better than that. You should be working on your self-esteem instead of settling for crumbs. Your pussy does not have a revolving door on it, so stop letting him fool you into thinking he will change if you take him back for the one millionth time!

Your ex is pissed off at you because you escaped the relationship. You weren't supposed to move on that easy. It doesn't work like that with a Narcissist. You're supposed to be crying, begging and pleading with him to come back to you. You're supposed to be blowing up his phone with text messages pleading with him to start over again. You're supposed to have your girlfriends drive by his apartment and spy on him. You're supposed to call up his mama or his best friend and tell them you still love him in hopes that they'll pass the message on to him. That's what the Narcissist wants you to do while he's out enjoying his new relationship. The sad part is, if you do end up chasing him, he will gossip with his friends and make a fool out of you.

But if you're a smart woman, you won't chase. You'll disengage and walk away. Let your ex be a whore and a headache to the new woman. Your ex will hate you for that. He wants total control over your life, even if he's not physically in it. He secretly gets off on seeing you in emotional pain while he's kicking it with his new supply. Real women do not cling. Real women do not tolerate abuse. Real women know their self-worth. Real women know when to walk away and never look back. Nothing good comes from dealing with an abusive man. His issues require the aid of a mental health professional who can properly diagnose him. The type of psychological assessment that your ex needs will require him to go to several years of intensive psychological therapy (*and we all know that the Narcissist is too arrogant to seek self-help, so forgot about him*).

Don't believe a single word that comes out of his mouth! It's all lies and fabricated delusions of grandeur that will never be. Save yourself the time and embarrassment. Move on. Create your own beautiful future.

STDs

(Sexually Transmitted Demons)

Narcissistic men are promiscuous scoundrels. They are polyamorous and have a crazy, insatiable appetite for sex; they're always on the prowl for new pussy (*and dick*). The Narcissist will hide behind their mask of fake machoism. He does not give a fuck about using protection, no matter how many sexual partners he engages. The Narcissist will continue to spread his trashy penis, sharing his rotten semen and dirty bodily fluids with whomever opens their legs (*or ass cheeks*).

When was the last time your ex went to the doctor to get his blood tested for sexually transmitted diseases and a full blown physical exam? Let me tell you right now, he's not going to give you an honest answer, because he's counting on you to go to the doctor on his behalf. If you test clean, then he figures he's clean too. This ignorant motherfucker doesn't even realize that HIV and Herpes can lay dormant in your body with no signs of any symptoms at all.

Sadly, your ex does not care about his health and by now you should know that he never cared about yours. If you continue to sleep with him after you break up, then my sister, you have some serious psychological issues. I don't care how good the dick is, ain't no man on God's green earth, worth the risk of you losing your life to AIDS.

As if putting your life at risk isn't enough, the Narcissist also dumps his toxic energy into your body every time you have sex with him. He is not only depositing his sperm into your vagina up inside of your cervix, he's also releasing spiritual residue from all of his ex-partners, into your temple. This is how demonic strongholds are created. Lust is often confused for love and emotions can run high when you're having orgasms on a consistent basis. Oxytocin and Dopamine are chemicals in the brain that are released from your body during/after sex. The Narcissist uses this to his advantage, manipulating every woman that he captures in his bed. He bases his self-worth on his accumulation of sexual partners (*Narcissistic Supply*) and the quality of each woman he chooses to use for money and other perks.

He manages to convince all of his fuck buddies that he's fallen in love with each and every one of them. This is why it's so hard for you to distinguish lust from love, because your ex used his "*Oscar Award-*

winning" acting skills to make you fall in love with him. He has no other way of making a deep connection with you (or any other woman) other than through sexual intercourse. He is an empty, shallow, heartless robot. What seems to be a man in love with you, is actually a manipulative low life, using his poverty penis and pillow talk to get you to become his personal servant. Women use sex to achieve love. Men use love to achieve sex. Nothing more or less.

The easiest way to catch feelings for someone is to have sex too soon before you solidify a concrete foundation. You both have to build a solid friendship first and be equally yoked before you decide to intertwine souls. Sex is not meant to be wasted on the unworthy, so why would you continue to sleep with a demon?

That's why you have to be careful with whom you share your body with. You'll find out later after you've broken up with your ex, that severing that soul tie can be a real motherfucker. You are actually entangled with a demonic entity. You keep a strong support system of spiritually-intuitive people around you at all times and stay prayed up. Your ex's demonic spirit is on a mission to murder your spirit. Ask God to deliver you and protect you from the aftermath of a Narcissist. Psalm 23.

God, Goals & Glam™

I decided one day to sit down and write out a list of short term and long term goals. No matter how much it hurt, I told God that I would remain obedient and faithful. I asked God to forgive me before I forgave myself and all of the people who had ever abused me. I stopped having pity parties and I faced the mirror to begin the process of cleaning up my life. I wanted to desperately make positive changes that would permanently impact my spiritual purpose forever. I didn't have time to focus on anyone else anymore. I wanted to design a blueprint to get my life back on track after my last relationship had failed. I was on a quest to re-invent myself and restore my dignity. I created a blue print that would forever change the outlook of my life: "**God, Goals & Glam.**"

#1. **God first**. There were days when I didn't feel like getting out of bed because I was depressed after I had found out that my ex was having unprotected sex with random women behind my back. That shit hurt like hell and it cut me deep. The crazy shit was that I never asked him to be in a relationship in the first place, he asked me! He told me that he wanted to marry me and actually tried to get me pregnant. I was in the middle of securing multiple grants to go towards the down payment of the purchase of our first home together when I caught him cheating. God pulled me up out of that shit right on time!

I did everything I could to make my ex happy and he still found a reason to complain **ALL OF THE DAMN TIME**. The more I gave him, the more he would gripe. The more love I showed him, the angrier he'd become. I never met a man so fucking ungrateful and miserable in all of my life. He never showed me any appreciation for supporting him unless it was beneficial for him to do so. I stood by his side through thick and thin when he couldn't turn to nobody else in his times of need. I took a lot of shit off of him.

Hindsight is always 20/20 and I had to forgive myself for not leaving him sooner. I will never tolerate this type of blatant disrespect from a man ever again. It's not worth my sanity or my finances. The depression isn't worth it either. I had to call on God to pull me out of bed. I had to call on God to give me the motivation to go to church to ask my pastor to pray with me after service. I had to call on God to give me the strength to go to work on the days I didn't feel like going. I had to call on God when I couldn't call on my family or friends. God never fails. My Lord and Savior was there the entire time watching over me while my bastard of an ex-boyfriend was busy destroying me. God allowed me to make my own mistakes before He intervened and saved my life. He saw the abuse I endured and He wasn't going to allow me to stay stuck in the dysfunction for long. If don't know anything, I do know that He loves me and He doesn't want nobody trying to harm me.

It took me a long time to realize that I was partially to blame for enabling my ex to hurt me the way that he did, but in hindsight, I realize it was more so him projecting his misery onto me. I had come to learn on my own that my ex-boyfriend suffered his own abuse from unresolved childhood issues that he endured from his mother and father. He is very angry for a lot of things that took place before I entered his life. I was made into his emotional punching bag during his fits of rage and temper tantrums. He has never taken the time out to go to therapy to address his tainted childhood and ongoing relationship issues. He has so much inner turmoil and baggage to clean up. He has no business being in a relationship until he fixes himself because he's definitely broken. He will always be toxic to anyone who attempts to love him. He will never take accountability for the destruction he has caused to many women or the long trail of broken hearts he has left behind him. Instead of him doing the therapeutic work to bring himself the proper closure to resolve those anger issues, he rather jump from relationship to relationship taking his frustrations out on the women he dates. He rather gamble his problems at the casino. He rather drink himself silly and have unprotected sex with multiple people. He rather vent to his Mommy all day because he's knows that she's not going to tell him to grow the fuck up. He seeks out his enablers and removes himself from reality. This is called *Escapism* (Indulging in various addictions, distractions and relief from unpleasant realities, especially by seeking entertainment, and/or engaging in fantasy).

I used to be angry at him, but now I feel nothing but sorrow for him. It must really suck for him to look in that mirror every day feeling inadequate, envious and miserable because his mother fucked up his outlook on relationships with women. I pray he gets the help he needs. He didn't deserve to be abused as a child and he needs to stop taking that

pain out on women. He's really angry at his
mother, but he can't separate her from the women
he's screwing over. He equates all women as one,
so therefore he abuses them as such. Until my ex
seeks his own intensive therapy, he will continue to
hurt quality women. I doubt that he ever will.
He's damaged goods.

It was never my job to teach him how to be a man.
I'm not a caretaker and that's where I went wrong in
my relationship. I've learned that you can't help a
broken man who refuses to help himself. Hurt
people will continue hurt people.

Thank God I dodged that bullet! Put God first no
matter how hard or difficult things get and He will
show you favor. You will rise from the ashes, but
you must stay persistent and consistent! You have
to learn the lesson before you can receive the

blessing. Put God first, and never put another man above Him ever again! Remember, we serve a very jealous God. He will send you a husband when He feels you're ready. Stop searching and learn to be happy on your own. God will show what real happiness is. All you have to do is stand in the light and receive the power of His love.

#2. Goals for now. So now that I stopped focusing on my ex, I am now plotting my victorious comeback. I sought counseling and set out to work on the broken parts of my life that I had previously ignored during my last relationship. My inner child needed healing.

Throughout my own journey with therapy, I was able to reevaluate my childhood issues as well. I learned that I was a codependent who was attracting abusive men into my life because my parents were both Narcissists. I never took the time out to deal with the trauma that they both had inflicted on me. They groomed me from the time I was born to be the scapegoat child of the family. I was conditioned to tolerate and accept abuse. I was forced to grow up and raise my siblings at the age of seven. I had no childhood because I was stripped of mine. By the time I became an adult, I was programmed to attract toxic people into my life. I was a people pleaser and a doormat. I didn't love myself or feel that I was worthy of love.

I had no idea that there was a clinical name for this kind of abuse that I had suffered. Therapy really helped me to dig deep and identify these behaviors and connect with them in order to heal. I was relieved that I finally knew what my diagnosis was. It was because of this abuse, that I was carrying my codependency issues into every relationship and repeatedly getting stomped all over by abusive men. I buried that pain into my romantic relationships and looked to my partner(s) to create my happiness. Reality check: nobody can create your happiness except you. I had to learn this the hard way because my parents didn't teach me to love myself. I had to also hold myself accountable for lowering my standards and trying to fix a broken man. I realize now that none of my ex's wanted to be "fixed." A broken man will always be content with wallowing in his own misery and dysfunction. A Narcissist will praise you for your achievements and he will envy you for them at the same time. The lesson that I learned throughout this turbulent journey is that no matter how much of a good woman you are, no matter how many degrees you have, how many people you take care of or how big your heart is, you cannot fix a broken man. A broken man has to be able to look in the mirror and fix himself.

If he refuses to clean up his act and treat a good woman right, then he must live with those consequences for the rest of his life. You have to leave before he gets a chance to fuck up *YOUR* life. Trust me, he's only going to break and destroy every other woman that comes into his life after you. The sad part is, he will never hold himself accountable for his part of the downfall of all of his ruined relationships. He will just continue to use and abuse new victims, one after the next. Wash, rinse and repeat.

I'll say it again, until he marries you and gives you his last name, he is not worthy of you. Do not claim him until you exchange wedding vows and are on your way to your honeymoon. And even then, go with caution (seriously). The sad truth is that you can be a loyal, faithful and supportive girlfriend and still get cheated on. Men don't know what they want until they are really ready for what they want. We think men are confused creatures, but they are not. If he's confused about whether or not he should marry you, then you're not the one for him. A man in love will not confuse you. It's as simple as that. Focus on yourself and don't become a cheater just because you were cheated on. Do the intellectual ground work to heal yourself in order to achieve the long-lasting results that will lead you to inner peace. You will soon attract a quality man of sound moral and spiritual principles into your life. Someone who vibrates on the same frequency as you do.

If you have survived a tumultuous break up with a Narcissist, then you should be working on rebuilding a stronger and wiser you. All throughout that toxic relationship, you ignored your needs in exchange for serving his. You gave up the things you enjoyed in order to please your ex, yet he still complained. You forgot who you were in the process of trying to satisfy an ungrateful man. It's time that you get back to your life.

What makes you unique? What hobbies do you enjoy? When are you planning to go to the club with your friends (*your real friends who want to see you win at life*)? Have you finished college? Do you want to start a business? Can your credit score use some improvement? Have you considered painting your apartment with new vibrant colors and redecorating? Have you tried yoga or rollerblading? Do you want to travel the world more often? Have you tried parasailing? What makes *YOU* happy? Write down a list of things that you've always wanted to do, and set a timeline to follow them through. Ignore all distractions. Focus on your goals and stick to them like glue. I don't care if you're broke, there are free activities in your city and/or volunteer positions to keep you busy. Stay on the path that God has placed before you and never allow any distractions to take you off course. Your life will fall into place once you commit to finishing your goals and placing men on the backburner.

#3. Glam forever. Once your goals have been set in stone and you're focused on rebuilding your future, then you can pamper yourself a lot more and start to become your "own" best friend again.

It's time to get a facial, a new hair style, and a new wardrobe. Stop by Sephora and stock up on some new cosmetics. Get a bikini wax! Take advantage of that discounted gym membership. Get your mind, body, spirit and finances in order.

If you want to start eating vegan, now is the time. Change your eating habits for the better. Try herbals and natural remedies to cleanse your intestines. Try a coffee enema to cleanse out your liver. Acupuncture relaxes you and does wonders to restore your energy levels. Hit the spa for a day of rejuvenation. Stock up on your favorite perfumes and nail polish. Buy a pretty dress and a pair of Louboutins. Treat yourself out to dinner. You've earned it and deserve it! Make a vow to yourself to never accept abuse from anyone ever again. Glam up baby girl because you deserve to spoil yourself. Stop waiting on somebody else to come along and do it. Treat your damn self!

The point I'm trying to make is, the Narcissist will do everything in his power to break your confidence once you've escaped the relationship. He has a malicious way of making you feel inadequate and he will do everything in his power to hurt you and pull your self-esteem down. Don't allow him to make you feel insecure, ugly or unloved.

Never settle for less ever again. Keep your legs closed and get to know every man you meet on a spiritual and intellectual level before you jump the gun and sleep with him too fast. Glam up your inner and outer beauty. Shine like the diamond that you are. He didn't break you. He broke himself when he lost control of you! Remember that.

God first. Goals for now. Glam forever. ♥

The Empath's Prayer

Heavenly Father, I come to You today broken, worn, weak and depressed. I don't understand this torment or abuse. I don't know why someone with whom I love with all of my heart, would want to destroy me like this. I do believe that You have created me with love and perfection in Your very own eye sight. You didn't create me to be abused. I ask that You forgive me as I learn to forgive myself. I ask that You protect me and help me to heal from this abuse. I pray for my enemies. I pray that You will lift this anger off of me. I will continue to pray during the times I become angry whenever I think about my abuser(s). I will continue to focus on loving You and loving myself. I will continue to have faith that all good prevails over evil and nothing goes unnoticed on Your watch. Help me to heal oh Lord. I also pray that you heal others as well. We are all fighting personal battles for we are in the midst of spiritual warfare. I choose to turn over my fears to You. I choose happiness. I choose my health and sanity over anything demonic. I ask that you rid my life of all toxic people. I ask that You cleanse my residence of any demonic entities and negative energy so that I can coexist in a safe environment of peace and tranquility. I choose you Lord. I will continue to pray for my enemies while You aide me in restoring my strength, my health, my happiness and my finances. I won't give up on love because I know in my heart that You are love and Love will always conquers all. I will wait patiently for You to send me that love, because I love myself even more. In Jesus name I pray. Amen.

Made in the USA
Middletown, DE
15 August 2023

36807391R00086